# Box Turtles as Pets Handbook for Beginners:

*Detailed Guide on How to Effectively Raise Box Turtle as Pets & Other Purposes; Includes Its Care& Diseases Plus Remedies; Feeding;Its Home & So On*

By

## Markus J. Muench

# TABLE OF CONTENTS

# CHAPTER ONE

## INTRODUCTION

Box turtles basically live ashore, and they can be fairly testing pets. They are a drawn out duty, living for quite a few years, in addition to getting their condition right can be troublesome.

Again, what are box turtles? Box turtles, by definition, are moveable creatures that rely on the lower shell that permits them to withdraw inside the shell and afterward totally close up, leaving no tissue uncovered.

American box turtles can be wonderful and amicable pets. Lamentably, a significant number of these magnificent creatures kick the bucket in view of helpless consideration. Kindly don't take box turtles from nature. Their numbers are decreasing a result of territory misfortune and weight from the pet exchange. Pet stores sell wild got turtles solely, so these ought to likewise be dodged.

There are a few types of box turtle, and each has varieties in its lodging and dietary needs. Some incline toward moister walled in areas than others; some need higher temperatures; some prefer to luxuriate, and one assortment even favors bitter (somewhat pungent) water to new.

Local to North America, the basic box turtle has a high-domed upper shell that is basically earthy colored designed with yellow or orange. It includes a somewhat little head with a snared upper jaw and will in general be an intriguing pet with a particular character.

We have two species as well as eight subspecies in North Americathat you should know:

Towards the eastern portion of the United States, you will discover the

Terrapenescarolinaspecies which incorporates the accompanying subspecies: The Three-Toed, Gulf Coast, Florida as well as Eastern Box Turtle.

For some specialist herpetologists these types of turtle can be high-support when contrasted and fledgling reptiles. They do require some lighting and high temperatures (which we will examine later on). Nonetheless, with some basic direction on diet and environment, and an everyday cultivation standard, thinking about your turtle turns out to be more typical and simple.

This reptile enjoys absorbing themselves water and investing energy outside on a radiant day. They are common omnivores, eating a wide assortment of spineless creatures, organic products, and vegetables. Known for being a generally solid creature, they can live to 50 years of age.

One of the numerous reasons apprentices decide to embrace this species is on the grounds that they are normally manageable, which makes them simple to deal with. They additionally endure every species inside their vivarium, so you can keep multiple!

**Species outline**

-Logical name: Terrapene Carolina

-Normal name: Common box turtle

-Grown-up size: 4 to 7 inches, and weighs 400 grams on the average

-Price: A little less than $50

-Future: 20 to 40 years (or more)

The next chapters will reveal all you need to know regarding**BOX TURLES as pets**from *a to z; care, feeding, housing, diseases and remedies, and lots more.*

# CHAPTER TWO

## BASIC BOX TURTLE CONDUCT AS WELL AS ITS TEMPER

Box turtles aren't viewed as reasonable pets for small kids or for new pet proprietors. This is because of their intricate consideration necessities, just as their weakness to push, which can extraordinarily influence a turtle's wellbeing. Hope to invest your energy cleaning and keeping up their fenced in area in any event week by week, just as taking care of them consistently or two.

Box turtles like consistency in their environmental factors, and most favor not to be taken care of by individuals. They don't regularly nibble, yet nervousness from over handling can lead some to nip an individual. Besides, they can convey salmonella, so it's critical to altogether wash your hands in the event that you do deal with your turtle or anything in its condition. When they're agreeable in their condition, most box turtles will figure out how to perceive their guardians, in any event, following an individual's developments from inside their fenced in area or asking for food.

**Lodging the Common Box Turtle**

Box turtles do best in a turtle-safe open air pen that copies their indigenous habitat, as long as temperatures don't fall under 50 degrees Fahrenheit. The pen ought to have dividers that are at any rate 18 inches tall with a shade to keep the turtle from moving out. It ought to incorporate bright and obscure territories, spots to cover up, and admittance to a shallow water dish. Besides, it ought to be shielded from predators.

In the event that you can't keep your turtle outside all year in your atmosphere, attempt to do as such for at any rate part of the year. It's hard for indoor box turtles to flourish. Whenever kept inside, utilize a terrarium that is in any event 40 gallons. Numerous proprietors additionally turn plastic kids' pools, sandboxes, and other enormous tubs into indoor turtle lodging. An indoor arrangement will require impressive space and exertion to make the proper condition for a crate turtle. Plan to outfit the fenced in area with a warmth source, UV lighting, spots to stow away, a shallow water dish.

Box turtles may rest if their walled in area is permitted to drop in temperature or they are housed outside. Yet, before you permit your container turtle to sleep, you should guarantee it is healthy. In the event that an unfortunate box turtle rests, it probably won't wake up. That is on the grounds that substantial capacities delayed during hibernation, so box turtles that are debilitated will conceivably be not able to battle the disease while in their profound rest.


## Warmth


Normal box turtles require daytime temperatures of around 70 to 80 degrees Fahrenheit with a luxuriating spot that is around 85 to 90 degrees Fahrenheit. Around evening time, the temperature can drop to somewhere in the range of 65 and 75 degrees Fahrenheit. Select a lounging light, just as earthenware heat producers or other warmth sources, to help control the temperature.

## Light

UVB lighting is basic for box turtles to process the calcium in their eating regimens. Without it, they can create metabolic bone illness and even bite the dust. Box turtles need around 12 hours of UVB lighting every day either by means of characteristic daylight or an UVB light. When inside, make certain to kill the light around evening time to copy a characteristic day-night cycle.

## Stickiness

Box turtles lean toward a dampness level of around 60%. You can keep up this through day by day clouding, just as by utilizing a substrate that holds some dampness.

## Substrate

Substrate is the material that lines the base of your case turtle's fenced in area. It assists with keeping up mugginess and fulfills the turtle's craving to tunnel. Additionally, it can cause the walled in area look and to feel more characteristic. Accordingly, plan to utilize a substrate that imitates the turtle's indigenous habitat. Numerous proprietors decide on compound free dirt, leaves, and greenery. Layer it in any event 4 inches deep to permit your turtle to tunnel.

# CHAPTER THREE

## INSTRUCTIONS TO GET A BOX TURTLE FED, THEIR KNOWN DISEASES PLUS PICKING A BOX TURTLE

Box Turtles are omnivorous kinds of reptiles.
They eat a wide assortment of things in nature:

-Apples

-Night crawlers

-Mushrooms

-Slugs

-Creepy crawlies and different bugs

-Blackberries

-Snails

-Strawberries

-Creepy crawlies

This eating regimen fluctuates with the season and their environment. The Box Turtle will utilize their solid jaw to catch and smash their prey before gulping.

## Food and Water

Since box turtles are omnivores, they need a fluctuated diet. Keeping them outside permits them to enhance what you feed them with what's in nature. New vegetables, natural products, bugs, low-fat meats, and pinky mice are a few nourishments that can be advertised. There are additionally business slims down accessible for box turtles; however you should enhance those with new nourishments.

Spot the food on a plate, paver, or other surface to keep the turtle from ingesting its substrate. Most youthful turtles need taking care of like clockwork while a few grown-ups may eat each other day. Counsel your vet on the right extents for your individual turtle. Clean water in a shallow dish ought to be given consistently.

**Do I have to give my case turtle nutrients and minerals?**

Turtles have a more serious requirement for dietary calcium than phosphorus. It is prescribed by numerous veterinarians to *lightly*sprinkle (2 – 3 times each week) all food offered to the crate turtle with a calcium powder (calcium gluconate, lactate, or carbonate). A *light* sprinkling of a decent reptile nutrient mineral blend on the food is likewise suggested week after week; particularly on the off chance that it contains nutrientD3 or vitamin D3. Any enhancements ought to be tidied onto little bits of plates of mixed greens or clammy **nourishments and those parts took care of first to guarantee that the case turtle gets them.**

A typical issue found in pet box turtles is over-supplementation with nutrients (particularly nutrient D3) and minerals. Check with your veterinarian about the need to enhance your pet's eating regimen.

**How regularly would it be a good idea for me to take care of my box turtle?**

Most youthful turtles eat day by day, while more seasoned turtles can be taken care of day by day or each other day, contingent on the pet's individual craving.

What are a few kinds of plant material I can take care of my turtle?

Most (80-90%) of the plant material ought to be
vegetables and blossoms, and just 10-20% ought
to be organic products. Generally speaking,
anything dim green and verdant should make up
an enormous aspect of the eating regimen.
Yellow, red and orange vegetables can likewise
be incorporated. Maintain a strategic distance
from fiber-rich, supplement and nutrient lacking
light green vegetables including icy mass or head
lettuce and celery, as their synthesis is
fundamentally fiber and water with minimal
supplement esteem. The inward light shaded
pieces of certain vegetables are less nutritious
than the more obscure green external leaves.

Satisfactory vegetables that ought to speak to a high level of the eating routine incorporate collard greens, beet greens, mustard greens, broccoli turnip greens, horse feed roughage or chow, kale, parsley, Swiss chard, watercress, clover, red or green cabbage, flavorful, cilantro, kohlrabi, ringer peppers, green beans, escarole and dandelion. A lesser level of the eating regimen can incorporate prickly plant, different squash, sprouts, cooked yam, parsnips, okra, cucumber, asparagus, mushrooms, carrots, peas and corn. Organic product can incorporate apples, pears, bananas (with skin), mango, grapes, star natural product, raisins, peaches, tomato, guava, kiwis, and melons. Organic products that are especially solid incorporate figs (which are high in calcium), apricots, dates, raspberries and strawberries. Organic products might be eaten specially, are commonly mineral poor and ought to maybe be utilized sparingly as a top dressing. As a treat, blossoms, for example, geraniums, carnations, dandelions, hibiscus, nasturtiums and roses might be advertised.

Vegetables can be offered cooked or crude albeit crude is more regular and holds more supplements. Altogether wash all products of the soil. Blossoms can be local or bought from flower shops. Frequently, botanical shops toss out more established, shriveling blossoms. While these might be unsatisfactory available to be purchased to the general population, the flower specialist will regularly offer them to box turtle proprietors. It is astute to be certain that no synthetic concoctions have been applied to the blossoms or water.

Swiss chard, spinach and beet greens ought to be taken care of sparingly as they contain oxalates that can tie calcium and other minor elements, forestalling their ingestion. Diets made fundamentally out of these vegetables can prompt supplement insufficiencies. Alert ought to likewise be practiced when taking care of cabbage, kale or mustard greens, as these contain goitrogens; unreasonable admission of these things may prompt hypothyroidism.

Food ought to be introduced to your crate turtle in a shallow clean dish that isn't effortlessly disturbed. Vegetables ought to be finely cleaved and combined to guarantee a wide assortment of food types are eaten and debilitate the eating of a solitary favored food thing.

What are some worthy creatures based protein nourishments I can offer my turtle?

On the off chance that you and your veterinarian conclude that creature based protein sources are adequate, some suitable nourishments incorporate grasshoppers, crickets, mealworms, wax worms, silk worms, moths, slugs, night crawlers, tofu, and hard-bubbled eggs. Great, low fat canine food might be taken care of sporadically. Business reptile pellets, flying creature pellets, and trout chow are brilliant protein sources. Live prey, for example, crickets and different worms ought to either be raised by the proprietor, recovered from a close by field or bought from a pet store, snare store or reptile reproducer. Care must be practiced when gathering creepy crawlies, particularly from the home nursery, as composts and bug sprays can be harmful to turtles.

**Normal Health and Behavior Problems**

The most genuine infirmity among numerous turtles is metabolic bone infection because of lacking UVB presentation. This agonizing condition can prompt debilitated bones and passing.

Respiratory contaminations, generally from deficient stickiness, are likewise normal among box turtles. Indications incorporate wheezing, bodily fluid around the mouth and nose, dormancy, and an absence of hunger. On the off chance that your turtle encounters regular respiratory contaminations, it could be an indication of nutrient A lack. Abstain from taking care of icy mass lettuce to a turtle with a respiratory disease. The creatures love it, however it has practically no dietary benefit.

Box turtles additionally are inclined to parasitic diseases. (Hostage reared assortments are at a much lower hazard.) This sort of disease doesn't generally give evident indications however can be analyzed by a veterinarian who represents considerable authority in reptiles.

What's more, box turtles can get an agonizing condition known as shell decay, which is brought about by a bacterial or contagious contamination. The shell will seem split or dry, and it may transmit a horrendous smell.

**These sicknesses ought to get therapy by a veterinarian.**

## Picking Your Common Box Turtle

Around the globe, box turtle populaces are declining. Along these lines, numerous states have laws against keeping wild box turtles as pets. The populace decay is only one motivation to get a hostage reared pet box turtle from a legitimate reproducer or salvage association. Another valid justification is you'll have the option to find out about the turtle's history and any medical problems. In addition, wild-got turtles for the most part don't change well to bondage and regularly kick the bucket from pressure. Comprehend what to search for to guarantee you're embracing a sound turtle. Any knocks or redness on the shell, bodily fluid in the nasal territory or mouth, or shady eyes can show a turtle with medical issues. Additionally, ensure the turtle has a firm shell and no expanding on its body. It's likewise best to abstain from buying a container turtle throughout the fall or winter when it ought to be sleeping. Another condition as of now can cause additional pressure.

NOTE: Wash your hands thoroughly and properly, particularly after taken care of your turtles.

**Maladies**

What are a portion of the normal sicknesses of pet turtles?

Regular states of pet turtles incorporate Vitamin An inadequacy, respiratory maladies, abscesses, shell contaminations and cracks, and parasites.

What are the indications of these illnesses?

Nutrient A lack (hypovitaminosis A) happens from taking care of turtles a wrong eating regimen. Turtles took care of icy mass lettuce, an all meat diet, or low quality business abstains from food are probably going to create hypovitaminosis A. Lack of Vitamin A brings about changes in external layer of their skin as well as  in the very mucous films plusfleshly fluid creating structures of the mouth, eyes as well as upper respiratory parcel. Manifestations of Vitamin An inadequacy incorporate an absence of craving, dormancy, expanding of the eyelids (regularly with a discharge like release), growing of the ear (really an ear canker) and respiratory diseases.

In turtles, most respiratory contaminations are brought about by microscopic organisms and frequently are auxiliary to a Vitamin An inadequacy. Turtles with respiratory diseases may have overabundance bodily fluid in their oral pits (seen as air pockets in the mouth), nasal releases, laziness, loss of hunger, open-mouth breathing, and wheezing, and may extend the neck with every breath.

A boil is a discharge filled expanding inside a tissue of the body. In pet turtles, abscesses show up as hard tumor-like swellings anyplace on or in the pet's body. Reptile discharge is typically extremely hard and dry with the surface and consistency of curds. Abscesses regularly happen in the ears of turtles, and they show up as an enormous growing along the edge of the head simply behind the eye. Abscesses in turtles are frequently identified with nutrient An inadequacy.

Shell contaminations (shell decay) are regularly experienced in turtles. These bacterial or contagious diseases are frequently auxiliary to injury, consume, or chomp. A portion of these diseases can enter profound into the body of the shell, causing profound ulcers or pitting on the body of the shell.

Inside parasites, for example, roundworms are normal in pet turtles. By and large, parasitic contaminations cause no clinical signs; they are distinguished on a routine fecal assessment. In extreme pervasions, intestinal parasites may cause the runs or weight reduction.

How might I tell if my turtle is debilitated?

Indications of malady in turtles might be explicit for a specific illness, for example, nasal release on account of a respiratory contamination. All the more ordinarily, indications of ailment are vague, for example, a turtle with anorexia (absence of craving) and laziness, which can be seen with numerous illnesses. In the event that your pet turtle shows any deviation from typical, you ought to be concerned and plan a prompt assessment by your veterinarian.

## How are turtle ailments treated?

Nutrient An insufficiency is treated with either oral or injectable Vitamin A. Treatment should just be done under veterinary watch as hypervitaminosis An, a condition coming about because of the off base utilization and over-measurements of Vitamin A, can happen. Nutrient inadequacy demonstrates that your turtle's eating regimen must be amended or improved.

Respiratory contaminations are frequently brought about by microbes. A considerable lot of these turtles likewise have Vitamin A lack that requires treatment. Your veterinarian may need suggest radiographs (X-beams), blood tests and societies to decide the reason for the contamination. Treatment for respiratory contaminations includes anti-toxins, which might be given orally, as infusions, or perhaps as nose drops. Debilitated turtles may require escalated care, including liquid treatment and coercively feeding in the clinic.

Abscesses are dealt with carefully. The ulcer is opened, the discharge is depleted and the influenced tissue is flushed with a cured purifying arrangement. A culture of the canker might be expected to decide the kind of microorganisms that caused the boil. Skin prescription, oral or injectable anti-toxins may likewise be required.

Shell cracks can as a rule be fixed by your veterinarian. Contaminations can be trying to treat yet for the most part include distinguishing what sort of life form (microbes or parasite) is causing the issue, completely cleaning the shell and utilizing the proper anti-microbial.

Parasites are treated with the suitable deworming drug. The kind of parasite distinguished on the minuscule fecal assessment will figure out which medication is required.

In synopsis, it is significant that you look for guaranteed veterinary consideration if there is any deviation from typical in your pet box turtle

# CHAPTER FOUR

## THE PROS AS WELL AS CONS OF MAINTAINING BOX TURTLES

Well I have been running dry on thoughts as of later however I at last concocted something and I feel entirely positive about this one as it appears to be acceptable on paper.

Well right away I present the advantages and disadvantages of keeping turtles.

**Pros**

1 They are totally different

They are unique in relation to a normal pet reptile as they have shells and most are sea-going making them pleasant augmentations to any assortment.

2 They are engaging.

They are consistently planning some mischief whether it be burrowing or pursuing down prey or simply relaxing looking at the climate.

3 They have changed eating regimens.

Most turtles are pioneering eaters and will eat
pretty much anything you toss before them since
I've never met a fastidious turtle.

4 Huge assortments

They are lovely animals from the normal Red
eared slider to others; there is something for
everybody in the turtle world as there are turtles
that are only a couple of inches long and
approximately a couple of feet long.

## Cons

Presently I'm not going to lie turtles are horrible
pets as a rule despite the fact that I love them to
death so now I got to name a few cons.

1 People don't have a clue what they are getting
into.

Numerous a period have I met a proprietor who has no clue about what they are doing and I have an inclination that its the most noticeably awful with turtles individuals pushing these animals in 10 gallons with no warmth light and just turtle pellets its a genuine disgrace individuals are so misled.

2 They eat a LOT

Presently this may change from turtle to turtle however my person can experience food like there's no tomorrow especially red leaf lettuce and night-crawlers. Simply realize the amount they eat.

3 They need enormous walled in areas.

This is a big deal and generally the issue with most proprietors as even the littlest pet turtle that is ordinarily kept, the musk turtle, needs in any event a 20 long or thereabouts. My male red eared slider is at present in a 75 gallon tank and to be straightforward I think it fits him great however the greater the better.

4 They are not cuddly.

Out of the apparent multitude of pet reptiles turtles are most likely the least cuddly as they'd preferably lounge and eat throughout the day I've had dig for quite a long time with incalculable communication endeavors and its a no every time they are simply best taken off alone.

5 They are not for amateurs

Regardless of how much individual's thinking, they truly are not amateur's reptiles they are muddled, eat a great deal, and are simply exceptionally requesting for what it's worth. The main turtle id even consider to suggest for a learner is a musk turtle since it remains little yet other than that they are horrible first pets especially red eared sliders.

# CHAPTER FIVE

## HOUSING PLUS ADDITIONAL CARE FOR YOUR BOX TURTLE, AND OTHER FACTS

### Lodging

What sort of confine does my container turtle require?

Box turtles might be housed inside or outside, contingent on natural conditions and proprietor inclination, in a departure verification nook that guarantees the security of the creature (giving assurance from predators or different creatures). Examine the advantages and disadvantages of every choice with your veterinarian.

In the event that you decide to house your case turtle inside (which is more secure), a 20-gallon aquarium is typically satisfactory regardless, contingent upon the size of the turtle. As the creature develops, you may need to furnish it with a 60 – 100 gallon aquarium, or an extraordinary room or part of a room, so as to give the turtle abundant floor space to stroll around and investigate. Greater is better, but on the other hand is more to oversee! The confine ought to be all around ventilated and doesn't really require a defensive top except if it is to keep different creatures out.

Does my container turtle need bedding in his enclosure?

Substrate, or bedding material, ought to be anything but difficult to clean and purify and be non-poisonous to the container turtle if incidentally eaten. Paper, butcher paper, towels, or ideally Astroturf (or other indoor/open air covering material) is suggested. A few people recommend utilizing straw, peat greenery or hay pellets as box turtles like to tunnel. In the event that you are utilizing Astroturf, purchase two pieces and slice them both to fit the base of the enclosure. With two pieces, one is put in the enclosure and one is kept as an extra that it is in every case perfect and prepared to utilize. At the point when the Astroturf inside the enclosure gets grimy, you can supplant it with the spotless, dry piece. Clean the filthy turf with conventional cleanser and water, at that point purify with weakened blanch (1 section fade to 10 sections water) Avoid harsher items except if your reptile veterinarian affirms their utilization. In the wake of washing, altogether flush it and balance it to dry until required at the following confine cleaning.

Horse feed pellets can be utilized for bedding and are frequently eaten by the turtle, which is adequate. Evade sand, rock, wood shavings, corn cob material, pecan shells, and feline litter, as these are hard to spotless as well as can cause impaction whenever eaten by the turtle, either intentionally or coincidentally (if the food gets secured by these substrates). Cedar wood shavings are harmful to reptiles and ought to never be utilized!

What else do I need in the enclosure?

Common branches are appreciated by the turtle.
Ensure they are secure and won't fall onto the
turtle and harm it. Shakes sufficiently simple to
jump nearby in the pen likewise take into
account an additionally intriguing condition. A
concealing spot is valued by all reptiles.
Counterfeit or genuine, non-poisonous plants
can be organized to give a concealing spot, as
can mud pots, cardboard boxes, bits of bark,
half-domed empty logs and different holders
that give a safe territory.

You will likewise need to furnish a shallow dish
or container with an "incline", in which the crate
turtle can undoubtedly move all through for
dousing and drinking. Watch this holder intently
as they here and there poop in it; keep it
extremely spotless. You can utilize a comparative
shallow clean dish for food.

Turtles, similar to all reptiles, are ectotherms (additionally called wanton, this implies they rely upon outside or ecological wellsprings of warmth to keep up their body heat). They need a scope of temperatures inside the enclosure to direct their inward internal heat level. Natural temperature decides the action of the container turtle. They delayed down in cooler temperatures. A warmth source is essential for all reptiles. In a perfect world, the enclosure ought to be set up so a warmth slope is built up, with one zone of the tank hotter than the opposite end. Along these lines, the case turtle can move around its condition and warm or cool itself, as it feels essential. Buy two thermometers that can't be harmed; place one at the cooler finish of the pen and one at the hotter end, close to the warmth source. The cooler finish of the enclosure ought to be around 700-75 0 F (21 0 - 240 C), while the hotter end ought to be 90 0 - 100 0 F (32 0 – 38 0 C). A reasonable method to do this is to gracefully a central warmth source utilizing a 100-watt brilliant bulb with a reflector hood; then again, you can buy different kinds of warmth lights or fired warming components at a forte pet store. Utilize these warmth sources as coordinated. Your warmth source ought to be set OUTSIDE or more one finish of the confine with the goal that your turtle can't straightforwardly reach it, in this way forestalling inadvertent consumes. Around evening time, when dozing, additional warmth and light are redundant, as long as the temperature stays at 65 o – 70 o F (18 o - 24 o C). You should give your crate turtle an "evening time". In the wild, the evening time temperatures generally fall steadily.

A warming cushion might be put under one finish of the pen for warmth; talk with your veterinarian to get familiar with the right method to utilize them so you abstain from consuming your pet.

Shouldn't something be said about bright (UV) light? A wild reptile may spend numerous hours daily relaxing in the sun, engrossing bright (UV) light. This range of light is basic for the body to fabricate the nutrient D3 that the turtle requirements for appropriate calcium ingestion from the digestive organs. Nutrient D3 is made in the skin. Inability to give UV light can incline your pet to healthful metabolic bone sickness. This is an excessively normal and totally preventable state of pet reptiles is deadly whenever left untreated. The UV light ought to emanate light in the UV-B run (290-320 nanometers). UV-A light (320 – 400nm), albeit significant regarding conduct, doesn't help in the production of nutrient D3. Most bulbs sold for use in reptiles give both UV-An and UV-B.

The UV yield of these lights diminishes with age so they ought to be supplanted at regular intervals or as coordinated by the producer. For UV light to work, it must arrive at the pet in an unfiltered structure, which implies that you should ensure there is no glass or plastic between the pet and the light. The light ought to be inside 6-12 crawls from the creature all together for the pet to get any advantage. These bulbs are costly, yet worth the additional expense and frequently mean the distinction between a solid reptile and a wiped out or passing on reptile. Normal presentation to regular DIRECT daylight outside (unfiltered through glass) is energized and suggested at whatever point conceivable. At the point when outside consideration must be taken, give a concealed territory to the turtle to get away from the sun on the off chance that it picks. Your pet turtle ought to consistently be managed whenever taken outside to loll in the sun, to keep getaway or assault from other meandering creatures in the area.

Shouldn't something be said about open air lodging for my crate turtle?


On the off chance that you decide to house your turtle outside, it ought to be contained inside a break verification fenced in area. Ensure a concealed zone is given, just as a concealing territory. The fenced in area must give sheltered and secure control or regulation against predators and different creatures just as give escape from blistering sun and downpour. A few proprietors discover a kids' swimming pool to be a reasonable compartment. You can utilize Astroturf for covering material, in spite of the fact that grass, twigs, and other characteristic material will be fine on the off chance that they are changed every day. Evade cedar, as it is harmful to reptiles. Obviously, food and new water should consistently be accessible. Bring the case turtle inside if the temperature dips under 6ooF (16 oC).

Again, box turtles will in general do well either outside, or in a huge indoor walled in area. Numerous individuals do keep them in minuscule aquariums, yet it is a fairly miserable reality, as I would see it. One kind of indoor holder that really works very well is a huge Rubbermaid tub. Rubbermaid tubs and exceptionally constructed wooden boxes have a bit of leeway over glass aquariums in light of the fact that they have murky sides. Some container turtles will fanatically attempt to traverse the glass to get to the bigger territory that they can see on the opposite side. Others become scared by any movement in the room and won't unwind until the sides are secured.

In the event that you live inside the regular scope of any of the American box turtles, you ought to genuinely think about an open air arrangement with sun, conceal, an assortment of weeds, and a little lake of water that is profound enough for swimming. Turtles are more joyful and more beneficial under these conditions. Some sort of insurance is needed to forestall raccoons, canines, or different predators from entering the nook.

Substrate:

Again, one substrate that functions admirably is a mix of gardening soil, sand, and leaf mulch and sphagnum greenery. At the point when moistened each day, it holds stickiness well. An item called "Bed-a-Beast" is suggested by numerous individuals for a similar explanation.

Tunneling into the substrate as well as stowing away under an empty log or "cavern" or the like causes box turtles to feel secure. Only a little cardboard box will work fine, however an assortment of logs and surrenders are sold at many pet stores. You ought to likewise make the substrate profound enough for the turtle to tunnel totally under.

Level rocks in a single zone will help keep the turtle's toenails fit as a fiddle.

All crate turtles need high moistness. Dry air can cause eye disturbance and even respiratory ailment. It can truly slaughter a crate turtle. Indeed, even the supposed desert box turtles give a valiant effort to stay away from dry air. They tunnel into clammy soil and come out at day break and sunset when dew soaks everything at ground level, and become exceptionally dynamic in downpour. Altogether fog the terrarium consistently. Your turtle is probably going to be generally anxious to eat directly in the wake of being moistened. Keeping pruned plants in the terrarium will offer a soothing characteristic look, and furthermore help keep up high dampness.

Water:

Box turtles appreciate swimming and absorbing water, so give a type of pool. They will regularly poo in their water compartment, and that helps keep the fenced in area clean, if the water is supplanted every day. Box turtles kept inside ought to be put in water to douse each day. Box turtles might be awkward swimmers, yet a large number of them do appear to appreciate it if a more profound lake is accessible in an open air nook. Some case turtles will swim in an outside lake for longer than an hour pretty much every warm day. Others simply swim and absorb the shallow end. Ensure there is a simple exit so a swimming box turtle doesn't become exhausted. Additionally, cool water can debilitate a turtle that falls in or enters to swim. A warm water lake with a simple leave will be valued by numerous American box turtles and represents no huge threat of suffocating.

Taking care of:

American Box turtles are omnivores and will appreciate organic products, parasites, veggies, greens, mollusks, worms and bugs. From research with wild turtles, we realize they eat plants for practically a large portion of the eating regimen and creature nourishments for a smidgen over a large portion of the eating routine. They are pioneering feeders, ready to eat nearly anything consumable that they find. So center on utilizing a wide assortment of nourishments. Feed the turtle on a level stone as opposed to from dishes of any sort. This more normal methodology will keep the bill and toenails from getting congested. Give a high calcium source constantly - for example cuttlebone, bubbled eggshells, mortar block- - so the turtle can chomp when it feels the requirement for more calcium.

In the event that your turtle is hesitant to eat, have a go at drenching and moistening before taking care of. Ensure the turtle is sufficiently warm, and well lit. Hesitant feeders can frequently be lured with live food, for example, a worm or slug, or bright nourishments, for example, strawberries or melon. Stinky nourishments, for example, canned feline food, can be helpful in getting a hesitant turtle eating. (In any case, feline food is definitely not a decent nourishment for regular use.) Sick turtles will normally not eat well, so if the turtle won't eat for over about fourteen days, look for veterinary consideration.

To act as an illustration of a decent, solid dinner for a case turtle, attempt a serving of mixed greens of hacked grapes, dandelion, and ground carrot, and include a wonderful garnish of night crawler. This ought to persuade your turtle that you are a decent supplier. After several days, give a mushroom and a strawberry a shot a turnip leaf, with a couple sow bugs on top, softly embellished with calcium powder. Try not to utilize similar nourishment for two feedings in succession. What's more, you truly don't have to take care of an "adjusted supper" each time. Utilizing a wide assortment of nourishments after some time will adjust the eating regimen in a more regular manner.

Box turtles can get into undesirable "addictions" whenever took care of a similar food every now and again. Utilize a wide assortment of nourishments and don't take care of similar things two taking care of in succession. Dodge abuse of live wiggly nourishments, as this is a typical reason for meticulous dietary patterns. Furthermore, try to give cuttlebone or other wellspring of calcium, with the goal that the turtle can self-control calcium admission.

You'll discover more data about chelonian sustenance at this page: What Should I Feed My Turtle?

Lighting:

Great lighting is significant physiologically and mentally. Reptiles need admittance to coordinate daylight or a substitution wellspring of UV-B beams, for example, Reptile D-Light is accessible at pet stores. An extra brilliant bulb is required for its glow and light. Set the radiant bulb with the goal that it warms one region of the terrarium to about 85F. Permit another part of the living space to stay cooler. Turtles that don't see light for in any event 12 hours daily can quit eating and become latent. (Dark lights or other extraordinary lolling lights are redundant, regardless of what pet store sales reps may let you know.)

Temperature:

Box turtles get along nicely at a wide scope of temperatures. Inside, no extra warmth (other than a warming light during the day) is essential. Open air fenced in areas must give a path to the turtle to maintain a strategic distance from extraordinary warmth (substantial shade in any event one region, profound tunneling capacity, and a lake.) Twice day by day sprinkling might be required in hot, dry districts. In regions where short-term temperatures are probably going to dip under 60°F., a fired radiator (accessible at pet stores) may help keep the turtle agreeable in one region of the nook. Indoor natural surroundings ought to give a cool region and a warm zone. During the day, keep one zone at about room temperature (68-72F.) with a relaxing region as warm as 85 (most extreme). Overnight temps can drop to around 60 and 75 (greatest).

# CHAPTER SIX

## CONCLUSION

Box turtles can make great pets, yet keeping them solid will require time and cost. The turtle, itself, may not be costly, yet recollect that appropriately preparing the environment, providing quality food, and giving veterinary consideration will cost cash. There are numerous turtles accessible for selection in light of the fact that the proprietors didn't comprehend the time and cost important to appropriately accommodate a turtle. In this way, before buying

a turtle, give it cautious thought, and afterward
you might need to contact a turtle reception or
re-homing association, and give a deserted turtle
a truly necessary home.

**THE END**